The Call of Liberty

Marquis de Lafayette and the American Revolution

Joanne Randolph

ROSEN CENTRAL
PRIMARY SOURCE™

THE ROSEN PUBLISHING GROUP, INC., NEW YORK

Published in 2004 by The Rosen Publishing Group, Inc.
29 East 21st Street, New York, NY 10010

Editors: Scott Waldman and Kevin Somers
Book Design: Daniel Hosek
Photo researcher: Rebecca Anguin-Cohen
Series photo researcher: Jeff Wendt

Photo Credits: Cover (left), p. 14 Giraudon/Art Resource, NY; cover (right) illustration © Debra
Wainwright/The Rosen Publishing Group; title page, p. 6 © North Wind Picture Archives; p. 10 Guildhall
Art Gallery, Corporation of London, UK/Bridgeman Art Library; pp. 18, 29 Picture Collection, The Branch
Libraries, New York Public Library, Astor, Lenox and Tilden Foundations; p 22. The Detroit Institute of
Arts, USA/Gift of Dexter M. Ferry Jr./Bridgeman Art Library; p. 30 © Corbis; p. 31 Library of Congress
Manuscript Division; p. 32 © Retrofile

First Edition

Publisher Cataloging Data

Randolph, Joanne
  The call of liberty : Marquis de Lafayette and the American Revolution / by Joanne
  Randolph.
    p. cm. —(Great moments in American history)
  Summary: The Marquis de Lafayette and French soldiers join the Continental Army
  in defeating the British at Yorktown
  ISBN 0-8239-4368-2 (lib. bdg.)
  1. Lafayette, Marie Joseph Paul Yves Roch Gilbert Du Motier, marquis de, 1757-
  1834—Juvenile literature   2. Generals—United States—Biography—Juvenile
  literature   3. United States. Army—Biography—Juvenile literature   4. United
  States—History—Revolution, 1775-1783—Campaigns—Juvenile literature 5. United
  States—History—Revolution, 1775-1783—Participation, French—Juvenile literature
  [1. Lafayette, Marie Joseph Paul Yves Roch Gilbert DuMotier, marquis de, 1757-
  1834   2. Generals 3.Statesmen 4. United States--History--Revolution, 1775-1783—
  Campaigns   5. United States—History--Revolution, 1775-1783—Participation,
  French]   I. Title   II. Series

  E207.L2 R28 2004
  973.3'092—dc21
  [B]   2003-009080

Manufactured in the United States of America

CONTENTS

Preface

❧❦❧

*I*n 1774, a seventeen-year-old named Marie-Joseph Paul Yves Roch Gilbert du Motier de Lafayette joined the French army as a captain. Since his name was so long, he was also known as the Marquis de Lafayette. The next year, Lafayette learned that the English colonies in America had begun to fight for their independence from Britain. This fight was known as the American Revolutionary War. Lafayette decided that he wanted to join the colonists in their fight for liberty. France's King Louis XVI did not want Lafayette to go to America. However, Lafayette had already made up his mind.

Lafayette began by secretly making plans to reach America. He bought a ship that would carry him and his men across the Atlantic Ocean. Since everything was done in secret, Lafayette couldn't leave from France. Instead, he traveled to Spain on April 20, 1777. Then, he and his men sailed toward America.

Lafayette landed in South Carolina in June. On August 1, Lafayette met with George Washington, the leader of the Continental army, for the first time. The two became close friends during the Revolutionary War. Lafayette fought side by side with Washington in many battles. He proved he was brave and that he believed in the colonists' cause. In 1779, he traveled back to France to get help for the colonists in America. French soldiers came to America to help the Continental army. By the time Lafayette came back to America in 1780, the colonists knew he was a true friend. Lafayette will always be remembered for what he did in the colonists' fight for freedom. Yet it was his bravery and heroism on the battlefields of Yorktown that made him an American hero.

Marquis de Lafayette was born into a very wealthy family. He was given control of his father's castle and received a large fortune from his mother. Yet he was willing to risk his life and give his fortune to the Americans' fight for freedom.

Chapter One

TRAPPING THE BRITISH

Marquis de Lafayette wiped the sweat from his forehead. It was a hot September day in 1781. Lafayette was not used to the heat of late summer Williamsburg, Virginia. He looked in the distance toward the fort at Yorktown. The British commander, Lord Charles Cornwallis, and his troops were at Yorktown. For the past few weeks, Lafayette and his men had been chasing Cornwallis and his men across the state of Virginia. The British soldiers could now no longer run. Both sides were preparing for a large battle. Lafayette knew that Cornwallis was one of the finest commanders in the British army. However, every day, more colonists arrived to help in the fight. If Lafayette and the other leaders of the American army won the battle, it could mean the end of the American Revolutionary War.

Lafayette and his men began marching quickly to an area near the fort. However, he did not want his men to get too close. He knew it was not time for the battle to begin. Lafayette waited for more help to arrive. The sun was high in the sky. Lafayette hoped the sun's glare would make it harder for the enemy to shoot at his men.

Lafayette and his men kicked up dirt as they marched. The dirt stuck to their sweaty faces. Finally, he told his men to stop their march. Lafayette ordered his men to dig a trench in the area where they had stopped. Later, they could hide in the trench until the time came for them to attack the British. After several hours of hard work, the trench was ready. Lafayette and his men returned to Williamsburg for the night. That night, Lafayette and American general, Anthony Wayne, talked about their plans for the battle.

"We need to keep Cornwallis from gathering any supplies," said Lafayette. "Even with all of our forces, it will be difficult to win against six thousand British soldiers who have plenty of food and water."

"That is true," replied Wayne. "But if Washington arrives with more soldiers, the British will not be able to escape."

The men wrote a letter to the commander of the American army, George Washington, asking him for help. With Washington's help, the colonists were closer than ever to winning their independence.

Lord Charles Cornwallis was thought to be one of the best British generals of his time. Before Yorktown, he had won several major battles against the Continental army.

Chapter Two

WASHINGTON ARRIVES

On September 10, more American soldiers arrived in Williamsburg. They had been sent ahead by Washington to join Lafayette. Four days later, Washington himself arrived in Williamsburg. When Washington and Lafayette saw each other, they hugged warmly. "Now we will give Cornwallis something to worry about!" Lafayette said.

"Indeed, I hope we will, dear Lafayette. I am pleased to see that you are well. You have done a great job helping our country," Washington said as he clapped his friend on the shoulder. He knew that many of Lafayette's men had thought about leaving the army not too long ago. They had not thought the colonists could win. Lafayette had made the men agree to stay by telling them that without their bravery, the war could not be won.

The men spent the next several days digging more trenches and making walls of dirt for them to hide behind near the British fort at Yorktown. At one point, Lafayette saw some British soldiers moving quickly around their fort. He watched closely to see if some kind of attack was being planned.

"Men, men! Look over there. What do you suppose they are doing?" Lafayette asked the soldiers working closest to him.

"Do you think they will attack?" one of Lafayette's young captains asked. He put one hand on his bayonet. *Perhaps they will, but I'm ready for whatever battle lies ahead*, Lafayette thought. As Lafayette looked more closely, he realized that the British were not preparing to attack. Instead, they were leaving some of the areas surrounding the fort. Lafayette realized that the British didn't think their army was

strong enough to fight out in the open. They were moving closer to the fort so that their soldiers were not so spread out.

"One less hole we have to dig," Lafayette heard one of his men say under his breath. A group of one hundred men was sent to check out one of the areas that the British had just left. Another fifty went to check out another position that had been cleared.

The American soldiers took over the areas while Cornwallis's men fired at them. Lafayette was worried about the heavy firing of bullets and cannonballs that were constantly whizzing past him and his men. He reminded the young soldiers to do as much of their work as possible from behind walls or within the trenches. He worried about losing men before the fighting began—whenever that might be....

This painting, *Siege of Yorktown*, was made by Louis Charles Auguste Couder in 1836. It shows the three important leaders of the armies that fought the British. General Jean-Baptiste Rochambeau is in the center (pointing), Washington is the tall man next to him, and Lafayette is the next man over, standing behind Washington's shoulder.

Chapter Three

PREPARING FOR BATTLE

As September turned into October, Lafayette and the other American leaders kept busy preparing for the battle. More than anything, they wanted the war to be over. They waited to attack until they were sure they could win the battle. In spare moments, Lafayette spoke with his men.

"Have you heard from your wife, Saunders?" Lafayette asked one of his men. "Any news of the little one being born?"

"Yes, sir. We have a new boy," replied Saunders. "A fine lad, my wife Lindsey tells me. She named him George after our great general."

Lafayette thought, too, of his own wife, Adrienne. She was back in France caring for their children. He thought sadly of his little girl, Henriette, who

had died while he was in America. Lafayette wanted the Americans to have their independence more than anything else. However, he missed his family. He understood that many of the young men fighting for liberty felt the same way. His soldiers were willing to risk their lives for their country. Yet they were also willing to be away from their families for long periods of time. Lafayette turned back to his work. There was still a lot to be done before any of them could go home.

Washington spoke with Lafayette every now and then, but for the most part, they were both busy preparing for the battle. The heavy cannons were in position. Ammunition that would be needed for the battle was brought and stored in the areas where the Americans would be attacking Yorktown. Men continued to dig ditches. They also shoveled dirt into mounds that they could hide behind during the fighting. The soldiers spent time cleaning their guns and sharpening their bayonets.

On October 6, Washington gave his orders to Lafayette and the other leaders. He told them how he wanted to organize the attack on the fort. He explained who would be in charge of each part of the battle. Washington wanted everyone to know what he was expecting. If his men were not organized, they would lose. If people acted on their own, they could be killed. Worse yet, the whole plan could fail. Washington made sure that everyone understood his orders.

Lafayette felt ready for the battle. He was a little disappointed that Washington had not given him more men to command. However, Washington explained that because Lafayette was French and younger than some of the other officers, he couldn't receive a higher position. Lafayette understood what his friend was saying. One of the biggest battles of his life was about to happen. There was no time to question any of Washington's decisions.

This occurred on the 14th. Two days after, Lieutenant-colonel Abercrombie made a sortie from the garrison with indifferent success, while during the same afternoon, the two captured redoubts were included in the second parallel, and one hundred pieces of heavy ordnance were brought to bear upon the enemy's lines. As the works of Cornwallis were now almost in ruins, he resolved on making his escape to New York by land, and had actually landed a portion of his army on Gloucester Point, when a heavy storm dispersed his boats, and the design was necessarily abandoned. Next day, several new batteries being opened, the works were no longer tenable; and his lordship requested of Washington a cessation of hostilities for twenty-four hours. The American commander granted him two hours, presenting at the same time a rough draft of propositions, on which he was willing to base articles of capitulation. Commissioners were appointed to digest these into form; and on the 19th Washington despatched the corrected copy to his lordship, expressing the expectation that they would be signed by ten, and the garrison be ready to march out by 2 P. M. of the same day. It being impossible to obtain better terms, Cornwallis was reduced to the mortifying necessity. The capitulation was signed at Moore's house, and at the appointed hour the garrison marched out, with their colours cased, and surrendered to General Lincoln on the same terms which, under similar circumstances, had been granted to that officer by Cornwallis at Charleston. Yorktown and Gloucester, with their garrisons and stores, were given up to the United States; the shipping and seamen

This page is from *An Illuminated History of North America, from the Earliest Period to the Present Time*, published in 1856. The drawing shows Lafayette leading his soldiers at Yorktown.

Chapter Four

The Roar of the Cannon

Washington and the other leaders decided on a signal that would let the soldiers know when the battle had begun. The American flag would be raised above one of the wooden walls the colonists had built to hide behind during the attack. They were told to fire their cannons and guns as soon as they saw this signal.

On October 9, 1781, around noon, the flag was raised. All the colonists' guns boomed at once. Lafayette was amazed at the loudness of the noise made by the cannons. He wondered how the British must feel behind the walls of Yorktown. Lafayette knew from his own battle experiences just how scary it was to see a flaming cannonball fly overhead. The sound itself was enough to make even the bravest man shake a little.

The men were firing the cannons at a house being used by Cornwallis as an office. It didn't take long for them to blast away most of the building. Cornwallis had escaped without being hurt, but the colonists' gunfire kept him worried. The British cannons fired back heavily.

Over the next week, the exchange of gunfire was constant. The number of dead and wounded increased each day. Yet Lafayette did not have time to hide from the continuous gunfire. He had to make sure his men stayed organized. If the Americans slowed down their attack on the British, they would surely lose the battle.

Soon, Washington called for Lafayette. The commander wanted to take over two of the dirt mounds the British were hiding behind. The dirt mounds had a wall around them and sharp wooden poles sticking out of them. To attack, Lafayette and his men would have to first break through the wall and then climb past the sharpened poles on the mounds. The entire time they attacked, British soldiers would be

firing at them. Lafayette would command the American troops to attack the mound on the left. A group of French soldiers would attack the one on the right. Lafayette felt proud to have been chosen. He left Washington to tell his men about the plan. He let them know they would attack the night of October 14. A cannon would fire three times. That would be their signal to begin.

That night, the men gathered as darkness fell. They lay on their stomachs as they waited for the signal. This way, the enemy would not see them.

When the three cannonballs were fired around eight o'clock, Lafayette and his men rushed the wall that surrounded the dirt mound. The fighting was close and gunfire was thick. Some men had been armed with axes. They quickly cut through the wooden stakes. They then ripped a hole in the wall, allowing Lafayette and his men to rush through and onto the dirt mound behind it.

Artist John Trumbull painted *The Surrender of Cornwallis* in 1787. The painting shows Cornwallis on his horse (center), Washington and his troops (right), and British troops with a white flag of surrender (left).

Chapter Five

THE BATTLE ENDS

"If we can take over the British positions on these mounds, the fort will be easier to attack!" Lafayette cried. "Rush in and attack!" Lafayette's men listened to their brave leader and rushed behind the wall. The noise from the guns was deafening. The air was filled with smoke. It was difficult to see. After a short yet hard battle, Lafayette and his men were able to take over the British mound. Lafayette called to his assistant. "General Rochambeau's soldiers, who are attacking the other mound, are being led by Baron Viominel. Send word to him. Tell him that we have captured one of the British positions. Ask him how he has done."

The assistant hurried off. In a short time, he returned with Viominel's message: "Tell the

Marquis that I have not yet taken over my mound, but I will be able to in five minutes." Lafayette had lost eight men in the attack. Another thirty had been wounded. The French group under Viominel had over fifty men who were killed or captured.

More American and French soldiers hurried to positions Lafayette and Viominel's men had just taken over. They were very close to the fort now. At about 4:00 A.M., the British attacked. They shot cannonballs at Lafayette and his men. Then the British Lieutenant Colonel Robert Abercrombie rushed out of the fort with four hundred British soldiers. They fought with the French troops. The British killed several soldiers and broke a cannon. But the French fought hard and soon beat the British back into the fort.

The Continental army fired on Yorktown the next morning. Their cannonballs did much damage. Soon, the walls of the fort began to fall down.

In the afternoon, one of Lafayette's assistants ran up to him. "Look, sir!" the youth cried. "The British are coming out of Yorktown." He pointed toward the enemy lines. A British officer was leaving the fort. In his hand was a white handkerchief, a signal that meant the British were giving up!

"We've done it then!" Lafayette said. By the end of the day, Cornwallis and Washington made a deal. The eight thousand British soldiers were to be taken as prisoners of war. After the war, they would be allowed to go home. The British turned over all their weapons to the Americans. Lafayette, Washington, and the other American leaders had just won one of the most important battles of the American Revolutionary War. Washington asked Lafayette to stand at his side to watch as the last British soldiers left the fort.

A few months after Lafayette and his men fought at the battle of Yorktown, the British leaders realized that they could not continue the war. It was costing them too much money

and too many of their men had been killed. People in Britain wanted the war to be over. Over the next year, more and more of the British left the American cities they had taken over. The British no longer had the strength to stop the Americans.

Finally, in September 1783, the British agreed to leave America for good. They would treat America as an independent country. America had won its liberty. When Lafayette received news that the war was over, he made plans to return home to his family in France. He was sad to leave George Washington and America. He had made many friends. Yet he looked forward to seeing his beautiful wife and his children.

On the day Lafayette sailed for France, he looked back at the country he fought for as it disappeared in the distance. He remembered the battle of Yorktown and all the brave men there who had given their lives so that others may live freely.

GLOSSARY

attack (uh-TAK) to try to beat an enemy or take over a place where an enemy is

bayonet (BAY-uh-net) a long knife that can be fastened to the end of a rifle

cannon (KAN-uhn) a heavy gun that fires large metal balls

colonies (KOL-uh-neez) territories settled by people from one country and controlled by that country

colonist (KOL-uh-nist) someone who lives in a newly settled area

commander (kuh-MAND-uhr) someone who controls a group of people in the armed forces

independence (in-di-PENS-duhnss) freedom; the condition of being free from the control of other people or things

liberty (LIB-ur-tee) freedom

positions (puh-ZISH-uhnz) places where someone or something is

trench (TRENCH) a long, narrow ditch, especially one used to protect soldiers in battle

wounded (WOOND-ehd) when a person is hurt by accident or from violence

Primary Sources

We learn about history by studying things such as photographs, letters, maps, diaries and drawings. By analyzing these sources, we can learn many important things about the people, places, and events of the past. For instance, the drawing on page 29 shows us how French soldiers dressed in the eighteenth century. By studying this drawing, we can compare and contrast the uniforms and equipment used by these soldiers to that of modern soldiers.

We can also use primary sources to evaluate the feelings a person or group may have had at a particular time in history. The check shown on page 32 shows us how thankful Americans were to Lafayette and how important they felt his role was in the American Revolutionary War. Sources such as these help us answer important questions about people who lived in the past.

This drawing of Lafayette's French soldiers who fought at Yorktown appeared in a book published in 1853. France also gave supplies and warships in the fight against the British.

This French map of the Americans' victory over Cornwallis at Yorktown was made in 1781.

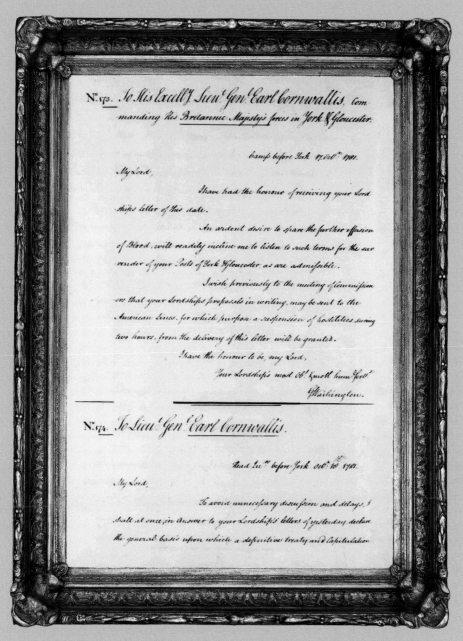

In this letter to Cornwallis, Washington asks for an end to the battle. Washington wanted Cornwallis to agree to stop fighting two hours after he received the letter.

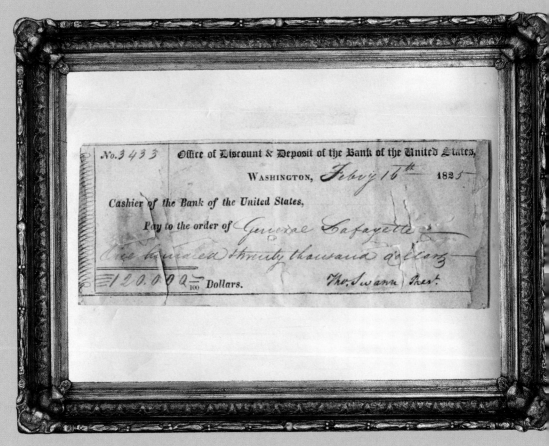

The American government thought that Lafayette was a very important part of their victory in the Revolutionary War. To thank him for his work, the government gave him this check for $120,000.